ANACONDAS

by Golriz Golkar

Cody Koala

An Imprint of Pop!
popbooksonline.com

abdopublishing.com

Published by Pop!, a division of ABDO, PO Box 398166, Minneapolis, Minnesota 55439. Copyright © 2019 by POP, LLC. International copyrights reserved in all countries. No part of this book may be reproduced in any form without written permission from the publisher. Pop!™ is a trademark and logo of POP, LLC.

Printed in the United States of America, North Mankato, Minnesota

042018
092018

THIS BOOK CONTAINS RECYCLED MATERIALS

Distributed in paperback by North Star Editions, Inc.

Cover Photo: ER Degginger/Science Source
Interior Photos: Shutterstock Images, 5 (top), 5 (bottom left), 6, 13; Steve Cooper/Science Source, 5 (bottom right); iStockphoto, 9; Yoshiharu Sekino/Science Source, 10–11; M. Watson/Science Source, 15; Sandro Campardo/Keystone/AP Images, 16; Gerard Lacz/Science Source, 19; Chris Mattison/FLPA/Science Source, 20

Editor: Meg Gaertner
Series Designer: Laura Mitchell

Library of Congress Control Number: 2017963421

Publisher's Cataloging-in-Publication Data

Names: Golkar, Golriz, author.
Title: Anacondas / by Golriz Golkar.
Description: Minneapolis, Minnesota : Pop!, 2019. | Series: Rain forest animals | Includes online resources and index.
Identifiers: ISBN 9781532160240 (lib.bdg.) | ISBN 9781635178197 (pbk) | ISBN 9781532161360 (ebook)
Subjects: LCSH: Anaconda--Juvenile literature. | Constrictors (Snakes)--Juvenile literature. | Rain forest animals--Juvenile literature. | Rain forest animals--Behavior--Juvenile literature.
Classification: DDC 591.734--dc23

Hello! My name is

Cody Koala

Pop open this book and you'll find QR codes like this one, loaded with information, so you can learn even more!

Scan this code* and others like it while you read, or visit the website below to make this book pop.

popbooksonline.com/anacondas

*Scanning QR codes requires a web-enabled smart device with a QR code reader app and a camera.

Table of Contents

Chapter 1

Big Snake

Anacondas are huge yellow, green, or brown snakes. They have spots and a black stripe on their heads. They have thick necks and narrow heads.

Watch a video here!

Anacondas spend time in water. Their eyes and nose are on top of their heads. They can breathe and look for **prey** while they are swimming.

Some anacondas weigh more than a piano!

Chapter 2

Slithering Along

Anacondas lie in the sun to get warm. Sometimes they hang from trees. They also **slither** into water, where they can move more easily than on land.

Learn more here!

Anacondas are **constrictors**. They hide in the dark water. They wait for an animal to come near.

Then they wrap themselves quickly around their prey.

They squeeze their prey instead of biting it. They eat fish, birds, and even deer. They open their jaws wide and swallow their prey whole!

After a meal, anacondas can go for months without eating.

Chapter 3

The Life of an Anaconda

Male anacondas struggle against each other for a **female**'s attention. Often the strongest male wins. Other times the female chooses the winner.

Complete an activity here!

Unlike most snakes,
anacondas do not lay eggs.
Instead, babies grow inside

the mother for six to seven months. The mother has 20 to 40 babies. Baby anacondas live by themselves. They live for about ten years in nature.

Chapter 4

A Snake's Home

Anacondas live in rain forests and swamps in South America. They live in wet, warm, and leafy areas.

Learn more here!

There are no animals that hunt anacondas. People sometimes get scared and kill them needlessly. People should leave anacondas alone to be safe.

Making Connections

Text-to-Self

Have you ever seen a snake at a zoo or in the wild? What did you think of it?

Text-to-Text

Have you read about other animals that swim? Why do different animals spend time in water?

Text-to-World

Sometimes people hurt animals when they are afraid. How can people become less afraid of certain animals? Where can they learn more about these animals?

Glossary

constrictor – a snake that kills its prey by wrapping tightly around it.

female – a person or animal of the sex that can have babies or lay eggs.

male – a person or animal of the sex that cannot have babies or lay eggs.

prey – an animal that is hunted, caught, or eaten by another animal.

slither – to move along the ground on one's stomach by twisting from side to side.

Index

Online Resources

popbooksonline.com

Thanks for reading this Cody Koala book!

Scan this code* and others like it in this book, or visit the website below to make this book pop!

popbooksonline.com/anacondas

*Scanning QR codes requires a web-enabled smart device with a QR code reader app and a camera.